# WILD RIDES

# Trucks and Diggers

An Hachette UK Company
www.hachette.co.uk

First published in Great Britain in 2012 by
TickTock, a division of Octopus Publishing Group Ltd
Endeavour House
189 Shaftesbury Avenue
London
WC2H 8JY
www.octopusbooks.co.uk

ISBN 978 1 84898 637 4

A CIP catalogue record for this book is available from the British Library

Printed and bound in China

10 9 8 7 6 5 4 3 2 1

Picture credits:
b=bottom; c=center; t=top; r=right; l=left
Ainscough Crane Hire: p.10-11, Alvey & Towers: p.4-5c, p.6-7c, p.24-25. Caterpillar: p.18-19c. Construction Photo Library: p.19t. Corbis: p.8-9. JBC: p.22-23. iStockphoto: cover, p.1. John Deere: p.28-29. Komatsu: p.12-13, p.16-17. Letourneau Inc.: p.14-15c. Mack Trucks: p.8-9. Oshkosh: p.20-21, p.26-27. Peterbilt: p.4-5.

Every effort has been made to trace the copyright holders, and we apologise in advance for any unintentional omissions. We would be pleased to insert the appropriate acknowledgments in any subsequent edition of this publication.

# Contents

Peterbilt 379 Road Truck........................ 4

Mercedes-Benz Actros ......................... 6

Mack Road Train................................. 8

Liebherr LTM 1500 Crane ................... 10

Haulpak 930E Dump Truck ................. 12

Letourneau L-2350 Wheel Loader ....... 14

Komatsu D575A Super Dozer.............. 16

Cat 385CL Excavator........................... 18

Oshkosh S-Series Mixer Truck ........... 20

JCB Backhoe Loader .......................... 22

Mercedes Tow Truck .......................... 24

Oshkosh Snow Blower......................... 26

John Deere 9750 Combine ................... 28

Glossary .............................................. 30

Index.................................................... 32

# Peterbilt 379 Road Truck

Peterbilt is one of the most famous names in trucking. The company's Peterbilt 379 was its flagship truck from 1987 to 2007, when the model was retired. The last 1,000 379s made were called the Legacy Class 379.

## DID YOU KNOW?

Many semi tractor-trailor trucks have a sleeping compartment at the back of the cab.

The massive engine sits in front of the driver, inside a long hood.

Always associated with quality, Peterbilt trucks are referred to as the Rolls-Royce of trucks.

**STATS & FACTS**

**LAUNCHED:** 1987

**ORIGIN:** US

**MAXIMUM POWER:** 600 BHP

**LENGTH:** 6 M

**WIDTH:** 3 M

**HEIGHT:** 3.5 M

**MAXIMUM SPEED:** 210 KM/H (130 MPH)

**FUEL CAPACITY:** 841 LITRES X 2 TANKS

**MAXIMUM LOAD:** 25 TONNES

**WEIGHT:** 12 TONNES

**WHEELBASE:** 5.94 M

The hood tips forward to allow easy access to the engine.

# Mercedes-Benz Actros

German manufacturer Mercedes-Benz makes the Actros cab-over lorry. A cab-over is built with the driver's cab positioned above the engine. This design is used in countries where a lorry's length is restricted.

## DID YOU KNOW?

Actros lorries are used to transport everything from dairy products to racing cars.

The 2012 Actros were revamped to offer almost every application needed for long-distance trucking. Redeveloped beds provide comfort when sleeping.

Wind can slow down a lorry. The Actros has roof spoilers to limit its effect.

Cab-over lorries link with semi-tractor trailers to carry goods. 'Semis' have no front wheels. Instead, they rest on the Actros' rear axle.

## STATS & FACTS

**LAUNCHED:** 1996

**ORIGIN:** GERMANY

**MAXIMUM POWER:** 460 BHP

**LENGTH:** 18 M

**WIDTH:** 2.44 M

**HEIGHT:** 3.5 M

**MAXIMUM SPEED:** 190 KM/H (120 MPH)

**FUEL CAPACITY:** 600 TO 705 LITRES

**MAXIMUM LOAD:** 29 TONNES

**WEIGHT:** 15 TONNES

**WHEELBASE:** 3.9 M

# Mack Road Train

Have you ever heard the saying 'built like a Mack truck'? These trucks are tough. Two or three trailers are linked together for long-haul transportation. The largest of all the Mack models is called the Titan.

The massive engine is cooled by a huge radiator.

## DID YOU KNOW?

Each model is built to the buyers specifications: they can choose everything, from size of the engine to the style of the sleeping compartment.

Mack trucks are known for their bulldog hood ornaments. The most powerful Macks sport a gold bulldog on the hood.

## STATS & FACTS

**LAUNCHED:** 1977

**ORIGIN:** US

**MAXIMUM POWER:** 600 BHP

**LENGTH:** 53 M

**WIDTH:** 4 M

**HEIGHT:** 3.5 M

**MAXIMUM SPEED:** 97 KM/H (60 MPH)

**TURNING CIRCLE:** UP TO 25 M

**FUEL CAPACITY:** 2 X 500 LITRE AND 2 X 265 LITRE TANKS

**MAXIMUM LOAD:** 120 TONNES (HIGHWAY); 240 TONNES (XHD)

**WEIGHT:** 14 TONNES

**WHEELBASE:** 5.26 TO 6.15 M

Large fuel tanks allow the truck to travel thousands of miles before refuelling.

# Liebherr LTM 1500 Crane

This Liebherr LTM 1500 is actually a crane on wheels. It can be driven from place to place. The arm (called the jib) extends like a telescope and can lift loads weighing as much as several cars!

## DID YOU KNOW?

The largest cranes in the world can lift a whopping 800 tonnes - that's as much as six blue whales!

Large fuel tanks allow the truck to travel thousands of miles before refuelling.

Cranes use lifting blocks to pick up weights. The larger the lifting block, the heavier the load it can hold.

An extra jib can be added to extend the crane's reach.

## STATS & FACTS

**LAUNCHED:** 2002

**ORIGIN:** GERMANY

**GROSS POWER:** 598 BHP

**CRANE ENGINE POWER:** 326 BHP

**LENGTH:** 21.6 M

**WIDTH:** 3 M

**HEIGHT:** 4 M

**MAXIMUM LIFTING HEIGHT:** 175 M

**MAXIMUM SPEED:** 80 KM/H (50 MPH)

**FUEL CAPACITY:** 600 LITRES

**MAXIMUM LOAD:** 500 TONNES

**WEIGHT:** 125 TONNES

# Haulpak 930E Dump Truck

Komatsu's Haulpak 930E Dump Truck is so big that it is not allowed to travel on roads or highways. It has to be taken apart and transported in pieces to a new site. Trucks like this are used in quarries and mines.

Sliding parts called pistons are used to tip the bucket up. The load then slides out.

## DID YOU KNOW?

As his seat is nearly 5 metres above the ground, the driver has to climb a set of stairs to reach the cab!

The engine is heavier than the weight of the loads this dump truck carries. This keeps the truck from tipping over as the bucket lifts.

## STATS & FACTS

**LAUNCHED:** 1996

**ORIGIN:** JAPAN

**MAXIMUM POWER:** 2,700 BHP

**LENGTH:** 15.24 M

**WIDTH:** 8.23 M

**HEIGHT:** 7.32 M

**MAXIMUM SPEED:** 65 KM/H (40 MPH)

**TURNING CIRCLE:** 30 M

**FUEL CAPACITY:** 4,542 LITRES

**MAXIMUM LOAD:** 325 TONNES

**WEIGHT:** 174 TONNES

**WEIGHT OF EACH TYRE:**
4.7 TONNES

# Letourneau L-2350 Wheel Loader

You could park a car in the bucket of LeTourneau's colossal L-2350 wheel loader. It holds the Guinness World Record for the biggest soil mover. Wheel loaders are used to shift mountains of earth and rocks into the back of dump trucks.

A pick-up, hoist and dump takes about 25 seconds.

## DID YOU KNOW?

Introduced in 2011, Generation 2 loaders are 50 per cent more fuel efficient than the competition.

The L-2350 is a real monster. Each tyre stands nearly 4 m tall. These are the largest mining tyres made.

A wheel loader's weight is low down. This stops the machine from turning over on sloping ground.

## STATS & FACTS

**LAUNCHED:** 2001

**ORIGIN:** US

**MAXIMUM POWER:** 2,300 BHP

**LENGTH (BUCKET DOWN):** 19.71 M

**BUCKET WIDTH:** 6.80 M

**HEIGHT (BUCKET RAISED):** 13.33 M

**TURNING CIRCLE:** 14.7 M

**GROUND CLEARANCE:** 0.5 M

**DIGGING DEPTH:** 0.25 M

**MAXIMUM SPEED:** 17 KM/H (10.5 MPH)

**FUEL CAPACITY:** 3,975 LITRES

**BUCKET CAPACITY:** 40.52 CUBIC M

**MAXIMUM LOAD:** 72 TONNES

**WEIGHT:** 190 TONNES

# Komatsu D575A Super Dozer

If a heavy object needs a push, a bulldozer is the machine for the job. Komatsu's D575A Super Dozer is the largest bulldozer of them all. These giants work in mines and quarries around the world.

Tracks help the bulldozer ride over muddy, uneven ground. The tracks are made up of links, which form a flexible band.

The Super Dozer is twice as big as any other bulldozer on sale.

## DID YOU KNOW?

This tractor crawler is available as a bulldozer/ripper or a dedicated bulldozer.

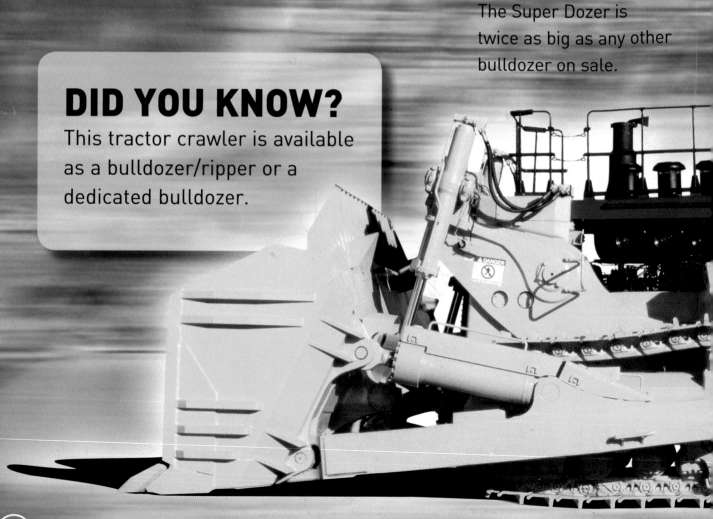

A Super Ripper attachment can tear up over 2,000 tonnes of earth and rock every hour.

## STATS & FACTS

**LAUNCHED:** 1991

**ORIGIN:** JAPAN

**MAXIMUM POWER:** 1,150 BHP

**LENGTH:** 15 M

**BLADE WIDTH:** 7.5 M

**BLADE HEIGHT:** 3.25 M

**NO. OF SHOES:** 49 EACH SIDE

**BLADE CAPACITY:** 69 CUBIC M

**MAXIMUM SPEED:**
FORWARD: 12.1KM/H (7.5 MPH);
REVERSE: 13.4 KM/H (8.3 MPH)

**FUEL CAPACITY:** 2,100 LITRES

**MAXIMUM LOAD:** 28.5 TONNES

**WEIGHT:** 76.54 TONNES

# Cat 385CL Excavator

Excavators are digging machines. Caterpillar produces everything from mini diggers to the giant 385CL shown here. A toothed bucket bites into the soil, then scoops and tips the contents into a dump truck.

The excavator's arm has three parts. The boom links the machine's body to the dipper. At the end of the dipper is the bucket.

## DID YOU KNOW?

The cheerful colour of these diggers dates from 1931. 'Highway yellow' made them stand out in traffic. It was also a response to the Great Depression, when many people were out of work.

The machine turns by stopping one of the tracks and continuing to move on the other.

## STATS & FACTS

**LAUNCHED:** 1991

**ORIGIN:** US

**MAXIMUM POWER:** 428 BHP

**LENGTH:** 13.08 TO 14.30 M

**BODY WIDTH:** 4.30 M

**CAB HEIGHT:** 3.80 M

**BUCKET CAPACITY:** 2.3 TO 4.5 CUBIC M

**MAXIMUM DIGGING DEPTH:** 6.94 TO 10.58 M

**MAXIMUM SPEED:** 7.1 KM/H (4.4 MPH)

**FUEL CAPACITY:** 990 LITRES

**MAXIMUM LOAD:** 4 CUBIC M

**WEIGHT:** 83.5 TONNES

# Oshkosh S-Series Mixer Truck

This mighty machine is the Oshkosh S-series mixer truck. It carries sand, gravel and cement. On the way to a construction site, water is added. The drum turns slowly to mix up concrete.

This cement mixer sends out concrete from the front. Its chute can be moved in any direction.

## DID YOU KNOW?

The mixing system used in this machine is 2,000 years old. It was invented by a Greek scientist named Archimedes. It is called the Archimedes Screw.

After the load is emptied, the inside of the drum is flushed with water. Any cement left inside would set and ruin this expensive machine.

Blades in the drum turn one way to mix the concrete and the other way to push it out.

## STATS & FACTS

**LAUNCHED:** 1999

**ORIGIN:** US

**MAXIMUM POWER:** 335 BHP

**LENGTH:** 12.2 M

**CHUTE LENGTH:** 6.68 M

**CHUTE WIDTH:** 4 M

**CHUTE HEIGHT:** 4.27 M

**MAXIMUM SPEED:** 80 KM/H (50 MPH)

**WATER CAPACITY:** 568 LITRES

**FUEL CAPACITY:** 190 LITRES

**MAXIMUM LOAD:** 10.05 CUBIC M

**WEIGHT:** 55 TONNES

# JCB Backhoe Loader

A backhoe loader digs trenches with its bucket. It then picks up the soil with its shovel and moves it out of the way. This machine is useful in all kinds of construction work all over the world.

JCB buyers can customise their machines. They choose the size of the bucket and the length of the arm.

## DID YOU KNOW?

Nearly half of all backhoe loaders sold are produced by JCB.

JCB has a team called the Dancing Diggers that performs stunts in a 30-minute show.

The operator swings the machine's arm around to work at the side of the loader.

## STATS & FACTS

**LAUNCHED:** 1962

**ORIGIN:** UK

**MAXIMUM POWER:** 100 BHP

**LENGTH:** 5.62 M

**WIDTH:** 2.35 M

**HEIGHT:** 3.61 M

**SHOVEL WIDTH:** 2.35 M

**MAXIMUM BACKHOE DIG DEPTH:** 4.67 M

**MAXIMUM SPEED:** 108 KM/H (67 MPH)

**FUEL CAPACITY:** 160 LITRES

**MAXIMUM LOAD:** 1.1 CUBIC M

**WEIGHT:** 7.5 TONNES

# Mercedes Tow Truck

When a truck breaks down, a tow truck takes it to be repaired. These gigantic trucks can haul two or three times their own weight.

Most tow trucks are equipped with floodlights because they often have to rescue vehicles at night.

## DID YOU KNOW?

Some tow truck are equipped with winches powerful enough to pull a barge up onto the shore.

Tow trucks are built to the buyer's requirements. This one was used to rescue tanks.

## STATS & FACTS

**LAUNCHED:** 1985

**ORIGIN:** GERMANY

**MAXIMUM POWER:** 600 BHP

**LENGTH:** 12 M

**WIDTH:** 2.44 M

**HEIGHT:** 5 M

**MAXIMUM SPEED:** 97 KM/H (60 MPH)

**FUEL CAPACITY:**
500 LITRES

**MAXIMUM LOAD:**
110 TONNES

**WEIGHT:** 20 TONNES

When a tow truck arrives on the scene, a strong metal shelf slides under the vehicle to be towed. It connects to the front wheels and winches it up onto the body of the tow truck.

# Oshkosh Snow Blower

A blizzard can cover a road in minutes. This Oshkosh snow blower helps keep roads and highways open to traffic by breaking snowdrifts into loose powder and blowing the powder off the road.

## DID YOU KNOW?

Attachments include sweepers, blowers and ploughs.

This machine has two engines. One drives the machine through snow drifts. The other operates the blower, which shoots snow off the road.

The high-speed HB series snow trucks move 5,000 tons of snow per hour at speeds of up to 55 km/h (35 mph).

The vertical exhaust pipes are protected from damage by a heat shield.

**STATS & FACTS**

**LAUNCHED:** 1991

**ORIGIN:** US

**DRIVE ENGINE POWER:** 505 BHP

**BLOWER ENGINE POWER:** 650 BHP

**LENGTH:** 8.52 M

**WIDTH:** 1.52 M

**HEIGHT:** 3.5 M

**MAXIMUM SPEED:** 73 KM/H (45 MPH)

**FUEL CAPACITY:** 2 X 473 LITRES

**WEIGHT:** 20.4 TONNES

**WHEELBASE:** 3.6 M

# John Deere 9750 Combine

In the 19th century, harvesting a small field took 10 workers a whole day. More workers then had to collect the crop and thresh it to remove the grain. Today, a combine harvester does the job in an hour.

The grain is stored in a large tank behind the cab. The cut stalks (the straw) are left in neat rows behind the combine so they can be gathered later.

## DID YOU KNOW?

When the tank is full, it can be emptied into the trailer of a waiting truck in a few minutes.

John Deere was a blacksmith, but in the 1830s he produced a highly successful steel plough. The company now produces equipment ranging from farm machinery to giant bulldozers.

The harvester cuts, collects, threshes and winnows. Cutting blades are 6 metres wide.

## STATS & FACTS

**LAUNCHED:** 1999

**ORIGIN:** US

**MAXIMUM POWER:** 325 BHP

**LENGTH:** 10 M

**WIDTH:** 6 M

**HEIGHT:** 5 M

**MAXIMUM SPEED:** 32 KM/H (20 MPH)

**FUEL CAPACITY:** 795 LITRES

**MAXIMUM LOAD:** 10,572 LITRES OF GRAIN

**WEIGHT:** 20.4 TONNES

# Glossary

**ARM** See boom.

**AXLE** The metal rod that joins a set of wheels.

**BHP** Brake horse power, the measure of an engine's power output.

**BLOWER** A machine for producing an artificial blast or current of air by pressure.

**BOOM** The back part of an excavator's arm, or a crane's long, extending arm.

**BUCKET** Scoop of an excavating machine.

**CAB** The part of a truck or digger that houses the driver and controls.

**CAB-OVER** A tractor unit in which the driver sits above the engine.

**CHUTE** A channel used to carry things downward.

**CONVENTIONAL** A tractor unit in which the engine is situated in front of the driver.

**DIPPER** The part of an excavator's arm between the boom and the bucket.

**DRUM** A metal container shaped like a barrel.

**ENGINE** The part of a vehicle where fuel is burned to create energy.

**EXCAVATOR** A machine that is used to dig large holes and trenches.

**EXHAUST** The pipe that carries waste gases away from an engine.

**FLOODLIGHTS** Powerful lights that are used to light up an area at night.

**HOIST** Part of a machine used for lifting.

**HOOD** The hinged metal covering over the engine.

**JIB** A crane's metal arm.

**PAYLOAD** The load a machine is paid to carry.

**PLOUGH** Machine used to turn earth so that crops can be planted.

**PISTON** A metal tube that slides in and out of a larger metal tube.

**RADIATOR** A device through which water or other fluids flow to keep the engine cool.

**SEMI TRACTOR-TRAILER** A truck that is made of two parts. It has a front tractor unit and a rear semi-trailer.

**SHOES** Metal plates that are attached to each link of a crawler machine's tracks.

**SHOVEL** A scoop used to lift and throw loose material.

**SPOILER** A raised panel that limits the wind's ability to slow a truck down.

**TANK** A large container used to store fuel or harvested crops.

**THRESH** The method of separating grain from its stalk.

**TRACKS** Two flexible metal loops attached to some vehicles in place of wheels. They help a vehicle to grip on muddy, uneven ground.

**TRACTOR UNIT** Name for a tractor's cab, engine and front wheels.

**TRAILER** A wheeled container pulled by a truck or tractor.

**TREAD** The grooves and ridges in a tire that help it grip the road's surface.

**TYRE** A rubber wheel covering filled with compressed air.

**WHEELBASE** The distance between a tractor unit's front and rear axles.

**WINCH** A machine equipped with a heavy rope or chain to lift heavy objects.

**WINNOW** The process of separating grain from chaff (straw dust).

# Index

## A

Actros 6, 7
Archimedes screw 20
axles 6, 30

## B

backhoe loaders 22, 23
buckets 12, 14, 18, 22
bulldozers 16, 17

## C

cab-over trucks
   6, 7, 30
cabs 7
Caterpillar, 385CL
   excavator 18, 19
combine harvesters
   28, 29
conventional tractor
   units 30
cranes 10

## D

Dancing Diggers 23
Deere, John, 29
   9750 combine 28, 29
Depression 18
diggers 18, 19
dozers 16
dump trucks 12, 13

## E

engines 30
   dump trucks 13
   road trains 8, 9
   road trucks 4
   snow blowers 26, 27
   tow trucks 25
excavators 18, 19, 23

## F

floodlights 24
fuel tanks 9, 13

## H

Haulpak, 930E
   dump truck 12, 13
hook blocks 11
horsepower 30

## J

JCB, backhoe
   loader 22, 23
jibs 10, 11, 30

## K

Komatsu 12, 13
   D575A Super
   Dozer 16, 17

## L

LeTourneau, L-2350
   wheel loader 14, 15
Liebherr
   LTM 1500 truck 10
   mobile crane 10, 11
   lifting blocks 11

## M

Mack
   hood ornaments 9
   Road train 8, 9
   Titan 8
Mercedes, tow
   truck 24, 25
Mercedes-Benz,
   Actros 6, 7
mixer trucks 20, 21

## O

Oshkosh
   snow blower 26, 27
   S-series mixer 20, 21

## P

Peterbilt, 379 road
   truck 4, 5
pistons 12, 30

## R

radiators 8, 31
road trucks 4, 5

## S

semi tractor-trailer trucks
   4, 5, 7, 31
sleeping
   compartments 4
snow blowers 26, 27
spoilers 7, 31
Super Ripper 17

## T

tanks 24
threshing 28, 29, 31
Titan 8
tow trucks 24, 25
tractor units 4, 7, 16, 30, 31
trailers 4, 7
tread 31
tyres 15

## W

wheel loaders 14, 15
wheelbase 31
winnow 29, 31